The Illustrated Story of President

JOSEPH F. SMITH

Great Leaders of The Church of Jesus Christ of Latter-day Saints

The Illustrated Story of President Joseph F. Smith
Great Leaders of The Church of Jesus Christ
of Latter-day Saints

Copyright © 1982 by
Eagle Systems International
P.O. Box 508
Provo, Utah 84603

ISBN: 0-938762-05-2
Library of Congress Catalog Card No.: 82-70687

Second Printing March 1983

First Edition

Lithographed in U.S.A.
by
COMMUNITY PRESS, INC.

A Member of
The American Bookseller's Association
New York, New York

The Illustrated Story of President

JOSEPH F. SMITH

Great Leaders of The Church of Jesus Christ of Latter-day Saints

AUTHOR
Della Mae Rasmussen

ILLUSTRATOR
B. Keith Christensen

DIRECTOR AND CORRELATOR
Lael J. Woodbury

ADVISORS AND EDITORS
Paul & Millie Cheesman
Mark Ray Davis
L. Norman Egan
Annette Hullinger
Beatrice W. Friel

PUBLISHER
Steven R. Shallenberger

A
Biography Of
JOSEPH F. SMITH

Joseph F. Smith, the sixth President of The Church of Jesus Christ of Latter-day Saints, has been described as an example of the "best character of the Mormon people. He was patient in trial, self-sacrificing, God-fearing, kind, able to withstand any hardship, and powerful in moral, mental, and physical strength."

This prophet of the Lord was born in Far West, Missouri, on November 13, 1838, to Hyrum Smith and Mary Fielding Smith. His was not to be an easy life. When he was a tiny baby, he was almost killed by some mobbers who attacked their home. His family was driven out of Missouri when he was a very small boy, and his father was murdered when he was only five. At the age of eight he drove an ox team from Nauvoo to Winter Quarters. When he was only nine, he climbed up on a wagon and drove another ox team over a thousand miles to the Salt Lake Valley.

His mother, Mary Fielding Smith, was a great inspiration to him. She taught him to read and study and to have faith in God. She taught him the power of prayer and to always give his best efforts to the work of the Lord. When the family arrived in the Salt Lake Valley in September of 1848, they had to live in their covered wagons for two winters until they could build a little home and begin to farm some land. During this time young Joseph did the work of a man to help his mother by plowing, harvesting, cutting trees, and tending animals. To Joseph's great sorrow, his mother died when he was only fourteen years old.

At the age of fifteen he was called on a mission to the Hawaiian islands. This was the first of several missions he served for the Church. Other calls were to England, to Europe, and twice again to Hawaii. He was ordained an apostle and a counselor to President Brigham Young when he was only twenty-seven years of age. He was later a counselor to three other presidents of the Church, John Taylor, Wilford Woodruff, and Lorenzo Snow. He was sustained Prophet and President of the Church on October 17, 1901, at the age of sixty-four. He was a tall, strong, handsome man, and some considered him to be the most powerful of all teachers of the word of the Lord.

He was forced to live in seclusion for seven years because of federal laws against plural marriage, but he was always a faithful and loving husband and a good father to his family.

The Church prospered during the presidency of Joseph F. Smith. All debts were cleared and fine buildings were constructed, such as the Church Office Building and temples in Canada and Hawaii. He also acquired Church historical sites, such as the Prophet Joseph Smith's birthplace in Sharon, Vermont, and the Joseph Smith farm in Palmyra, New York.

He died on November 19, 1918, just a few days after his eightieth birthday. It was said of him that no man who ever lived bore a more powerful testimony of the living God and the Redeemer. He testified fervently that Joseph Smith was a Prophet of God and that the Book of Mormon was a divine book.

The autumn of 1838 was a sad and perilous time for the Latter-day Saints. There were enemies all around them who were determined to destroy the Church. In October the Prophet Joseph Smith and his brother Hyrum were taken at gunpoint from their families and chained in jail in Richmond, Missouri. Only a few days later, on November 13, 1838, a son, Joseph Fielding Smith, was born to Hyrum's wife, Mary. The new mother was weak and ill and she longed to have her husband at her side, but both she and Hyrum were willing to give their lives, if need be, for the work of the Lord. Mary's sister, Mercy Thompson, and her children were staying with the Smith family to help care for the mother and her new baby.

Many weeks passed, and still Hyrum and Joseph were locked in jail. Then one night the wicked men who hated the Saints came very close to putting an end to the life of little Joseph F. Smith before it had hardly begun. It was a cold, wintry evening when Joseph was only about two months old. Suddenly Mary and Mercy were alarmed to hear shouting and cursing outside their home. The door was kicked open. Some mobbers burst into the house and pushed the frightened women and children into a corner of the room.

"Search the place, tear it apart!" one man yelled. Thereupon they pulled open drawers, broke into a trunk, and threw everything they could lay their hands on about the room. They did not notice the tiny baby lying on a bed. The ruffians picked up a mattress off the floor and threw it on top of the bed, completely covering little Joseph. When they had finished their destruction they rode off into the night. Mary Smith cried out, "My baby, my baby!" She frantically pulled the mattress off the little fellow. He was blue and nearly dead from the smothering. Fortunately he was still breathing and his life was miraculously spared, for the Lord had a great work for Joseph F. Smith to do in his kingdom.

The mobs would not leave the Saints in peace. Mary was still ill in bed when, for her safety, friends took her from Missouri to Quincy, Illinois. Her husband, Hyrum

finally escaped from his enemies and joined her there. How happy he was to be with his wife, his baby son, and others of his dear ones again! A few weeks later Hyrum took his family to Commerce, Illinois, to live. The small settlement of Commerce was later to become Nauvoo, the beautiful city of the Saints.

For a few years life was quite safe and pleasant in the city of Nauvoo. The Hyrum Smith family was often in the home of the Prophet Joseph. Sometimes little Joseph F. sat upon his Uncle Joseph's knee. But as the Church grew, troubles began just as they had in other places. Its enemies were determined that the religion and its people would be destroyed. Little Joseph did not understand, but he must have been uneasy as he saw the concern on the faces of his father, his mother, and his uncle, Joseph Smith.

One day when Joseph F. was five years old, he was standing by the road near his home. His father, Hyrum, rode up on a horse. "We have been ordered to go to Carthage to meet with the governor," he told his son. Then, without getting off his horse, Hyrum leaned over in his saddle and picked up the little boy. "Son," he said sadly, "I must leave you again. Be a brave boy and help your dear mother all you can." He kissed Joseph and held him close, then he gently set him on the ground. The boy watched as his father rode away. He probably felt the greatest sadness of his life without quite knowing why.

A few nights later Joseph F. was awakened from his sleep. Some of the Brethren were knocking on the window, calling to Mary: "Sister Smith, Sister Smith, we bring you sad news. Your husband has been killed!" Little Joseph sorrowed throughout the night, as he heard the sobbing of his mother.

Mary Fielding Smith was not physically strong, but she knew that she must prepare to leave Nauvoo. Early in the year of 1846 Joseph watched as some of the first Saints began leaving Nauvoo. As the wagons moved out, he called, "See, Mother, the wagons are crossing over the frozen river." "Yes," answered his mother, "we are no longer safe here. President Brigham Young has called the Saints to settle the mountains of the West." She continued, "Joseph, we too must gather together teams and wagons to follow them."

Mary prayed for help and worked hard and by summertime she had obtained ox teams and wagons for the journey. Mary knelt by her son. "Joseph," she said, "you are only eight years old, but I must depend on you. You will have to be a man before you are hardly a boy." Joseph bravely took charge of the ox team. "Get along there," he called to them, and thus began the two hundred mile trip from Nauvoo to Winter Quarters.

His mother sometimes said to him, "Joseph, I could not make this journey without your help and your faith." Joseph, in turn, admired his untiring and devoted mother. He noticed that she was brave and cheerful in spite of the hardships. He wanted her to be proud of him, so he was an eager student when she taught him to read, to study, and to have faith in the Lord.

When they arrived at Winter Quarters, Mary moved her family into a cabin and set about to make it as comfortable as she could. It was not long after this that Joseph learned a lesson he never forgot. It happened when Joseph, his mother, and her brother, Joseph Fielding, made a trip down the Missouri River to St. Joseph to buy food and other supplies for their journey to the West that was to begin the following spring.

They took two wagons, each pulled by a team of oxen. Joseph drove one team, his Uncle Fielding drove the other. On the trip homeward they camped one evening on a little open prairie close to the river. They turned the oxen loose in their yokes to feed on the grass. The next morning Joseph went to find the oxen. He ran back, calling, "Uncle Fielding, Uncle Fielding, one of our teams is gone!" Uncle Joseph Fielding was very concerned and said, "We cannot afford to lose our oxen. We must find them!" They both ran off to begin the search. They pushed through the tall grass, wet with dew.

Finally, discouraged and soaked to the skin, Joseph returned to the camp. There he came upon his mother on her knees. He heard her pleading with the Lord, "Please lead us to the oxen that we might continue our journey in safety. . . ."

14

Just as she arose from her knees, Uncle Fielding came into camp. "Well, Mary," he announced sadly, "the cattle are gone. They are not to be found." But Mary merely said cheerfully, "Never mind. Your breakfast has been waiting for hours. And now, while you and Joseph are eating, I will just take a walk out and see if I can find the cattle."

Joseph and his uncle looked at each other. "Why, Mary," Uncle Fielding exclaimed, "what do you mean? We have been all over this country and through the timber. Our oxen are gone! I believe they have been driven off, and it is useless for you to try to find them." "Never mind me," said Mary. "Eat your breakfast and I will see." She started toward the river.

A man who was herding cattle nearby called to her, "You are going in the wrong direction. I believe I saw your oxen over this way." Mary smiled but walked straight toward the riverbank. Suddenly she stopped and motioned for Joseph and his uncle to come. Joseph outran his uncle to where his mother stood pointing. There were the oxen, caught in a clump of willows down in a gulley. Joseph and his uncle quickly freed the oxen, and they were soon happily on the road again. Joseph thought about what had happened. "The Lord knew what we needed. My mother had faith that her prayer would be answered. And it was!" Always afterward he had an unwavering faith in the power of prayer. It was a source of comfort, peace, and guidance throughout his life.

THINK ABOUT IT:

1. Tell about some of the hardships of Joseph F. Smith's early life.
2. Relate an experience that shows how Joseph F. Smith developed faith in the power of prayer.

When the spring of 1848 arrived, it was time for the Saints at Winter Quarters to begin their long journey across the plains to the new gathering place in the valleys of the Western mountains. Mary Smith had joined with her sister, Mercy Thompson, and together they had done all they could to prepare for the trip. They had managed to gather together several old wagons, which they loaded with their belongings. They did not have enough cattle to pull them, but they would not give up! They hitched some of

the wagons together, then they yoked up their cows, calves, and oxen. One of the leaders said, "The Widow Smith will just be a burden to us. The men will have to spend too much time taking care of her and her party. The journey will be too difficult." Joseph heard him and thought, "He is wrong. I can do the work of a man. I will show him I can do all that is necessary!"

So they set out, full of faith, for the West. Nine-year-old Joseph was one of the drivers. All day he drove his oxen as they pulled the big, awkward wagons. In the evening he took care of the animals. He yoked and unyoked the teams. Sometimes he could see that the oxen were so weary they could scarcely move. He was a tenderhearted boy and would put his arms around their necks and weep for them. He took his turn at day guard, along with the men of the camp. He did all he could to show the men that his mother would not be a burden.

One day as the sun beat down on the company moving slowly through the hot sand and dust, one of their best oxen suddenly laid down on the ground, rolled on its side, and its legs began to jerk. It looked as if it would die on the spot! The captain of the company rode up, looked down at the ox, and said, "He is dead; there is no use working with him. We will have to find a way to take the Widow Smith along with us. I told her she would be a burden upon this company." But not so! Mary Smith came carrying her small bottle of consecrated oil and asked her brother, Joseph Fielding, and others of the priesthood to administer to the ox. Some people looking on may have whispered, "She has taken leave of her senses." But the men did as she asked, poured a few drops of oil on the ox's head, laid hands on him, and prayed for his recovery. Within a few moments the ox got up, stood blinking, and immediately traveled off with the other oxen. Once again Joseph had seen his mother's faith in action. He knew the Lord would take them safely to the Salt Lake Valley.

They finally arrived on September 23, 1848. Mary Smith set out at once to find a place for her family to settle. She and her children lived in their covered wagons for two winters until they were able to build a small home and begin to farm some land south of Salt Lake City. It was here that she taught Joseph another lesson—this time about tithing. She said to him, "Take our best loads of potatoes to the tithing office. The Lord's share must be the pick of the crop." She believed without doubt that they would be blessed by the sacrifice. Joseph noticed that they were indeed blessed. He said, "We never lack . . . we are never without cornmeal and milk or butter. . . ."

Joseph was responsible for the family herd of cattle. He was only ten years old, but he never lost an animal. Besides this he also helped plow the land and chop down trees, along with planting and harvesting.

But Mary Smith had more spiritual strength than physical strength and finally her health broke. Her family, particularly Joseph, grieved when this noble mother passed away on September 21, 1852.

Now here was Joseph, at fourteen years of age, with neither father nor mother. He sat alone and thought about what he should do. He felt frightened. He did not have much knowledge. What would become of him? Then he received powerful help from the Lord. Joseph dreamed he saw himself entering heaven, being greeted by his beloved mother and father, President Brigham Young, and the Prophet Joseph Smith. It seemed to him not a dream, but real. Later he told about his experience, "There could never be anything more real to me. I felt the hand of Joseph Smith. I felt his warmth when I put my hand against him. I saw the smile upon his face . . . I know that it was a reality, to show me my duty, to teach me something, to impress upon me something that I cannot forget. When I awoke that morning, I was a man, although only a boy. There was not anything in the world that I feared. I could meet any man or woman or child and look them in the face, feeling in my soul that I was every bit a man. That vision . . . and witness that I enjoyed has made me what I am, if I am anything that is good."

At the time of his vision he said to himself, "I will live so that both Mother and Father will be proud of me."

Joseph did not have to wait long to prove his faithfulness. During April conference of 1854 his name was read out as a missionary to teach the gospel to the people of the Hawaiian islands. Imagine a fifteen-year-old boy called to serve a mission in a faraway land with a foreign language! But Joseph was no ordinary fifteen-year-old boy. He had grown to be tall and strong. He had proven that he could take care of himself. He had a complete faith in the gospel of Jesus Christ. These strengths prepared him for his mission.

He set out by ox team for California, the youngest of a group of nine missionaries. They had to stop along the way to earn money to continue their journey, but they finally came by ship to the Hawaiian islands. Young Joseph listened to the natives as they talked to one another. He thought to himself, "Oh, how can I ever understand and speak this strange tongue." But he did! Because of his determination, he learned the Hawaiian language in only one hundred days. He became known as an exceptional missionary. Through the power of the priesthood he preached, healed the sick, cast out devils, and presided over several branches of the Church. The nine missionaries left Hawaii about three years after they had arrived. Joseph had reached the age of nineteen when the ship docked at San Francisco. The group traveled down the California coast and then started eastward across the desert to Salt Lake City.

One night Joseph and his companions were sitting around the fire at their evening camp when a group of Mormon-haters rode up. The leader shouted, "We will kill anyone who is a Mormon!" Then pointing his gun at Joseph, he demanded, "Are you a Mormon?" The brave young man said without hesitation, "Yes, siree; dyed in the wool, true blue, through and through!" The Mormon-hater was astonished. He shook hands with Joseph, "You have some courage there, young man," he said. Then he called to the other men, "Let's ride on!"

The day after Joseph arrived in Salt Lake City he enlisted in the legion to help defend the Saints against Johnston's Army that had been sent by the federal government to put down a so-called rebellion of the Saints. Joseph later told his friends, "I was constantly in my saddle prospecting and exploring the country between Salt Lake City and Fort Bridger [Wyoming]. I was on picket guard with a party of men under Orrin Porter Rockwell. When the army finally passed through the deserted city of Great Salt Lake, I helped my relatives return to their homes."

When Joseph F. Smith was twenty-one years old, he married Levira A. Smith. He said, "It is time for me to settle down and raise my own family." But again, in April conference of 1860 his name was read out to serve as a missionary, this time to England. He answered the call and drove a mule team across the country to New York City, where he boarded a ship for England. He proved himself once again to be an outstanding missionary. Some believe that it was on this mission that Joseph F. developed into an exceptional speaker. One historian wrote, "As a preacher of righteousness, who could compare with him? Of all the preachers of the Gospel, I always think of Joseph F. Smith as the greatest I ever heard—strong, powerful, clear, appealing. It was marvelous how the words of living light and fire flowed from him. . . ." Yet Joseph never thought of himself as being above other men. He was simple, humble, and unaffected. People were impressed by his dignity and said of him, "Here is a man among men!"

He sometimes talked about his boyhood. He said, "I was acquainted with the Prophet Joseph in my youth. I was familiar in his home, with his boys, and with his family. I have sat on his knee. I have heard him preach. From my childhood to youth, I believed him to be a Prophet of God . . . I [also] believe with all my heart in the truth of the Book of Mormon . . . and hope to be faithful to God and man, and not false to myself, to the end of my days."

He returned from England in September, 1863. He was overjoyed to be with his family again and said, "Now at last we can settle down." But once again President Brigham Young called him to serve the Lord. This time he was sent with two of the Twelve Apostles, Ezra T. Benson and Lorenzo Snow, to help solve some problems of the Church in the Hawaiian islands. He knew the language well and was able to help his leaders.

When he returned home, he worked for about a year and a half in the Church historian's office. Then on July 1, 1866, he was asked to attend a meeting of some of the apostles and President Brigham Young. As the meeting was ending, suddenly President Young turned to his Brethren and said, "Hold on! Shall I do as I feel led? I always feel well to do as the Spirit tells me." He paused, then continued, "It is in my mind to ordain Brother Joseph F. Smith to the Apostleship, and to be one of my counselors." It was probably a surprise to those in the room, and no doubt twenty-seven-year-old Joseph F. Smith was utterly amazed. But then and there he was ordained to this high office by Brigham Young. The Lord had inspired President Young. Joseph F. Smith, the little orphaned boy, grown to manhood, had proved himself through his faithfulness, his wisdom, and his untiring efforts. The Lord needed him to help guide the Church in the years ahead.

In 1873 he was called to preside over the European Mission. This was his fourth mission! He returned in the fall of 1875 and was again called to the European Mission in April, 1877. He had just arrived there, however, when President Brigham Young died in August, 1877. Joseph F. hurried home to work with the other Brethren to govern the Church.

On October 10, 1890, Joseph F. Smith was named counselor to President John Taylor. Later he also served as counselor to both President Wilford Woodruff and President Lorenzo Snow.

For a period of time during President Taylor's administration the leaders of the Church suffered greatly. They had practiced plural marriage, and the federal officials came to arrest them. For seven years Joseph F. Smith was in exile. He traveled among the settlements of the Saints in southern Utah, Colorado, Arizona, New Mexico, California, and once again in Hawaii. Finally in September, 1891, when the "Manifesto" stopped the practice of plural marriage, Joseph F. Smith was free to return home. He said, "This is a memorable day to me, and no words . . . can express my gratitude to God."

On April 7, 1893, a great event took place. The Salt Lake Temple was dedicated by President Wilford Woodruff. Joseph F. remembered that as a small boy he had watched the laying of the cornerstones. Now, forty years later, he watched as a counselor to the President of the Church when the building was dedicated to the Lord.

President Joseph F. Smith was a strong, vigorous man just one month short of his sixty-fourth birthday when President Lorenzo Snow died. Joseph F. Smith became President of the Church on Oct. 17, 1901. He was the first President of the Church to be born to Latter-day Saint parents.

Under President Smith's leadership the Church moved forward. It was cleared of debt and many fine buildings were constructed. He also acquired a number of Church historical sites, among them the Joseph Smith farm in Palmyra, New York.

Joseph F. Smith tried to live so as to be spiritually in tune with the Lord. One day when he was on a train returning from a trip to the East, he went out to the end of the car and stood on the platform. A voice said to him, "Go in and sit down." He went back into the train car and stood by his seat. He thought, "Oh, pshaw, perhaps it is only my imagination." He heard the voice again, "Sit down!" and he immediately took his seat. Just then there was a tremendous crash! A broken rail had thrown the engine off the track, and most of the cars were off the track and jammed up together. The passengers were badly shaken up, but President Smith's car stayed on the track. He would have been seriously injured or even killed if he had stayed on the platform of the car. President Smith told his companions, "I have heard that voice a good many times in my life, and I have always profited by obeying it."

At one time President Smith visited the Saints in Holland. A little blind boy named John heard of his visit and said to his mother, "If you will take me to the meeting and have the President look into my eyes, I know I will be healed." He had perfect faith. After the meeting President Smith greeted John kindly, then lifted the bandage, from his eyes and looked into them. Laying his hand on John's head, he promised, "The Lord will bless you." When John arrived home and took off the bandage, he was overjoyed. "I can see! I can see!" he cried. John and his mother thanked Heavenly Father for the healing power of a living prophet.

President Smith was greatly loved by the members of the Church. When they poured out their love and faith in his behalf, he said, "My heart is like that of a child. It is easily touched, especially with love. I can easier weep for joy than for sorrow. There is much to remember in my early years of pain and sorrow, so that now the confidence and love of my brethren and sisters goes directly to my heart. . . ."

One historian, Charles W. Nibley, who traveled often with President Smith, said of him, "Everywhere and on all occasions, I have found him the same great, brave, true-hearted, noble and magnificent leader, so simple and unaffected, so entirely democratic and unassuming. He loved a good story and a good joke. There was a good laugh in him always . . . he could entertain the crowd about him as few men ever could. He was fond of music and loved to sing the songs of Zion. His love for children knew no bounds. It was always a difficult task to pull him away from a group of little children. He wanted to shake hands with and talk to every one of them."

He was the kindest of husbands and the most loving of fathers. When his own little children were ill, he would walk the floor with them throughout the night.

At general conference in 1917, when he was seventy-nine years old, he told the people, "I begin to feel that I am getting to be an old man, or rather a young man in an old body. I think I am just about as young as I ever was in my life in spirit. I have the truth today more than I ever did before in the world. I believe in it more firmly now than I ever did before . . . I understand it better from day to day by the promptings and inspiration of the spirit of the Lord. . . ." It was said that no man who ever lived had a more powerful testimony of the living God and the Savior than Joseph F. Smith.

THINK ABOUT IT:

1. What were some of the exceptional strengths of Joseph F. Smith as a leader in the Church?
2. If President Joseph F. Smith could speak to the people of the Church today, what would he say to them?

Just after his eightieth birthday he became ill with pneumonia and on November 19, 1918, he died. The people of the Church mourned the loss of their beloved prophet and president.

His great friend, Charles W. Nibley, wrote of him at his death, "I can say of Joseph F. Smith . . . No heart ever beat truer to every principle of manhood and righteousness and justice and mercy than his; that great heart, encased in his

magnificent frame, made him the biggest, the bravest, the tenderest, the purest, and best of men who walked the earth in his time." No higher tribute could be paid to anyone.

President Joseph F. Smith, like the Prophet Joseph Smith, Jr., was truly a visionary "man among men."

TESTIMONY

I desire to bear my testimony to you; for I have received an assurance which has taken possession of my whole being. It has sunk deep into my heart; it fills every fiber of my soul; so that I feel to say before this people, and would be pleased to have the privilege of saying it before the whole world, that God has revealed unto me that Jesus is the Christ, the Son of the living God, the Redeemer of the world; that Joseph Smith is, was, and always will be a prophet of God, ordained and chosen to stand at the head of the dispensation of the fulness of times, the keys of which were given to him, and he will hold them until the winding up scene—keys which will unlock the door into the kingdom of God to every man who is worthy to enter and which will close that door against every soul that will not obey the law of God. I know, as I live, that this is true, and I bear my testimony to its truth.